Make

Your

Money

Find

You

The Millennial Handbook For Creating Massive
Wealth.

Dr Ayo Olu-Ayoola

Rights

This book came

by

Enore

(My wife) who never could get tired no matter who or
what tried;

for

Ayodola,

Ayofolalowo

and

Ayojolalo

(all loving sons)

Dedicated to

Prof. Ayobanji Ephraim AYOOLA (my DNA Dad)

And

Dr. Isaac Oluwabukola ALUKO (my VCN Dad)

Special Thanks

To Seun Ayoola and Auntie Bose wonderful editors that I could count on,

To Eganoyemi Adetayo, Peter Okosun and Harley Tawo sometimes I wonder if and how I deserve such immense dedication to me.

To Femi Adewumi, Ovie Okoh, Abiodun Adekanmi and Feyikemi Frederick you guys are the most awesome family of creatives

And finally to my wonderful friend Sam Harvard in whose house I was when I wrote this book. I am super grateful for the daily morning tea.

Table of Contents

Foreword

The Sign

We are always looking for a sign, something to confirm our biggest and deepest convictions. While you are alive, you desperately wish for something out of the ordinary, a message, an incident or a pattern. Everyone loves to have people look into their eyes and say, 'Wow, you are going to go far in life' or 'you are going to be a great person' or 'you know you are going to be wealthy.'

At various points in my life, I have had people say this to me, and I am not going to lie to you it felt good, even though the signs I got did not directly have any impact on my immediate months or years, but they filled me with a strong sense of auspiciousness. I went on thinking and feeling sure of being successful.

This book is much more than a sign; this book is your energy totem. Green lantern found the ring; Spiderman was bitten by a spider. Batman found a cave full of bats. You have found this book. Whomever you are (hopefully, you will write to me ayodamolaoluayoola@gmail.com so that I can know who you are), I want to tell you that I have always thought you will be super-wealthy and very successful, at this moment as I write this, I am more certain of it.

"This book is much more than a sign; this book is your energy totem. Green lantern found the ring; Spiderman was bitten by a spider. Batman found a cave full of bats."

Like you, I grew up wishing and looking for a sign, something external to confirm everything that I wanted to believe. I needed to know that I was special and that I was made for great things and I did get those signs from time to time. If you have been waiting for a sign, this is your sign. I am telling you now that you are going to do great things in life and you will make a lot of money while you are it. I am one thousand percent sure and in the course of this book, you will see how I have come to be so sure.

The Difference

I am glad that you are holding this book in your hands right now. You may have read many books about money, business, self-help, wealth creation; however, I would be happily surprised if you have ever read a book like this one that talks about your money.

Several other books will talk about opportunities and how to build businesses, but this book will tell you what your money looks like and answer that burning question of "if other people are already making the money that you are supposed to be making", I mean because at the moment, you are probably clueless and struggling against economic tides with your head just barely above the financial waters.

The Clarity

This book will change your life!

This is not because there are incantations in it, well come to think of it, there are incantations in it [Not the kind you see in West African Movies anyways], but because it will show you many things that you do not see. This book is not a magic wand but even a magic wand has to be wielded and used before it works. No magic wand works on its own. This book, however, will beam a floodlight on the very essence of your life.

Clarity is bliss; every form of clarity is pure unadulterated bliss. And you will be able to see everything that you have or own. This book will help you know what to do at this point in your life, to understand how to create a gusher of wealth for yourself, and, more importantly, to rid you of the fear of dying poor.

All honest entrepreneurs can tell you how they made their money, but most of them cannot tell you how you would mostly make yours. I can, and I am here to show you how you most likely will create your wealth. I am doing this because it is what I am supposed to be doing, and yes I am really interested in your overall wellbeing; I want you to have good success. I want you to prosper in physical health, mental health and material wealth.

"This book will change your life! This is not because there are incantations in it, well come to think of it, there are incantations in it [Not the kind you see in

West African Movies anyways], but because it will show you many things that you do not see."

Rest Easy

I am sure that you see a lot of successful people around you; some of them only seem to be doing better than you; some of them are doing it illegally. So before we move on here, the focus of this book is not about how you can do better than someone who is illegally doing better than you, you are already better than these sets of people. Decide now that you are better than them already because one day, not long from now all of that ill-gotten wealth will disappear and they will disappear like they never were here; now, that, my friend, is a given.

"This book is specially made for you. You are not sinking into a mire of hopelessness, never, not on my watch."

You are worried that people are already making the money that you should make, that they seem to be enjoying all the things you should be enjoying or thought you'd be enjoying by now. That feeling is crushing. I remember it. What comes to your mind is how old you are and how time is going, how you have not done all the things you thought you would have done by now. This book is specially made for you. You are not sinking into a mire of hopelessness, never, not on my watch.

"You are better than those who are ahead of you illegally"

12

The Guarantee

How do I know that I can help you? Because I have been there. As I talk a little about myself you may see a glimpse of yourself in me; your life is likely better than how mine was, it was as though all I knew to do was to make an already bad situation worse.

My life changed very rapidly for good. I can tell you all about it. But this book is about you, how did I know I should write this book? Well, I had wrongly assumed that the principles that helped me were something that everyone knew.

People would ask me what I did, why and how my life transformed. I would reply that I did not necessarily do anything. But that was, in fact, a lie. It was convenient though, the issue was that what I did was not something I could share in a momentary conversation. Not because it was a lot of volumes but because I had not sat down to articulate and put them down as clear thoughts or words. And yet people didn't stop asking me.

I realized then that this book needed to be written, and everyone has to read it. Some people may never meet me their entire life, but there are times in our lives that hopelessness visits us. I need to reduce as much hopelessness as I can. I expect that you and everyone else reading this book right now will never be hopeless anymore but rather go on to become a massive success story. And I want you to know that I feel honoured to be part of it.

"I realized then that this book needed to be written... I need to reduce as much hopelessness as I can. I expect that you... reading this book right now will never be hopeless anymore but rather go on to become a massive success story."

Chapter 1

Know Who You Are

Who Are You?

Sounds cliché but it is the foundation of any fundamental change to our lives. Eventually, the battle of the mind is that of identity. I believe that change is almost impossible without first identifying who you are and who you want to be.

The Need

"Why is it essential for you to be certain of who you are? Because how would you know what your money (if you already know what money is) looks like if you do not know who you are."

I am heavily weighed down inside of me as I sit at my desk to write this, knowing that you could fix almost everything wrong with you by just knowing who you are.

Let me challenge you right now. I am going to ask you a simple question. Who are you? I am sure the first thing that comes to your mind is your name. If I gave you a pen now, how many words do you think you would be able to write about who you are? At the end of this chapter, you will be able to clearly say who you are with as much detail as you want.

Why is it essential for you to be certain of who you are? Because how would you know what your money (if you already know what money is) looks like if you do not know who you are? Money does not know people's names, money knows who people are. You have not found your money because you do not even know who you are; every time you go out, your money would have come across you screaming, are you who you are? But since you did not know who you are, you could not scream, 'yes!' back at your money so your money continued its desperate search for "YOU".

When you know clearly who you are, you would be able to spot your money from several miles away, and you'd probably be the one to scream 'my money I am here!'

"When you know clearly who you are, you would be able to spot your money from several miles away, and ...scream 'my money I am here!'"

The Journey

Getting to know yourself is a journey; it is much of paying attention as it is embracing the truth, as it is (the truth). You do not know who you are because you have not been paying enough attention to yourself, today you will begin to pay more than enough attention.

Decide now that you will pay attention to who you are so you can know who you are. You came with a distinct pattern of fine lines on your palm and fingers, science calls it fingerprints, that is God trying to tell you that you are not anyone else, and then you have a distinct - separate-from-the-rest-of-the-world retina print, this is so you can know that no one else alive or dead or yet to be born has your DNA. I am trying to get it into your head that you are someone, that you are a distinct and entirely unique person; no one else will ever be you!

Now, pay maximum heed to what I am about to tell you. Today, you are going to find you. You are going to recognize you. And you are going to know you. I suppose you are alone in your thoughts right now, reading this.

I am going to work you through knowing who you are. Separation and comparison are the height of understanding, knowing who you are and who you are not. We are going to be using keys words like unique and exclusive.

I Am Here To Help

I am going to recount who I am to you, and I want you to mirror the process to find who you are. You are a finely woven wire meshwork of nature, nurture, and experience. You have to look at everything between your very beginning to where you are now; for people who have not been paying attention, it is a repeated letter from who you are to you.

As you mirror this process, pay attention to your experience, your perspective to things, what bothers you that seemingly does not bother anyone else, the things that only you seemed to understand and areas where you have been misunderstood.

"You have to look at everything between your very beginning to where you are now; for people who have not been paying attention, it is a repeated letter from who you are to you."

Before we start, you have to agree that nothing was a mistake, nothing that happened to you was ill-fated. Say to yourself, this is my life; this is my journey; this is me. I am nobody else; I am me, I am whole, I am different, and that's really a fine thing.

Chapter 2

How To Know Who You Are

To know who you are, there are people you must take a good long look at.

Your Father

(Pun present but not intended. You can ask Twitter Nigeria about it).

Look at your father, on writing this line the first thing that came to my mind is that some people do not know their fathers.

Have no fear, knowing or not knowing your father is where your journey starts. If you do not know who your father is, do you know that your first really (big) money may be helping other people find their daddies, or just giving them a platform to share their stories? Perhaps, that is how you were meant to be famous and popular. Perhaps, that is how you were supposed to help Daddies come out and find their abandoned or denied pregnancies turned children. Who is better equipped to run that package other than you?

Those who know their fathers will never understand what it feels like to (you probably realize right now that you know someone who falls in this category that you may need to talk to as soon as you finish reading this book - only God knows what he or she has gone through, usually something not many people talk about it, Oh gosh!) not know who your father is.

"...your money lies in the 'experience' 'You' can give other people."

We wouldn't know about all the tears that went into the pillows, all the muffled cries. We would not know all the things these people battle every day. But therein lies the irony, just imagine how much influence and money the owner of the 'father search' network could make on Facebook and Instagram or from videos of people on YouTube.

Imagine it as a big reality TV show. Imagine how much money a T-shirt franchises of "Your Daughter somewhere needs you" "Your Son needs you right now", "I am only a bastard because my dad went to hide", "I wish my Dad would see how much I look like him", "Go find the child you left" could make.

Imagine how much healing one person's pain could gift the world. Whew! I have jumped ahead of myself a lot! But that's okay too, Let me keep jumping ahead of myself and say, you are not about you, your money lies in the "experience" "You" can give other people.

"The number of people you serve is directly proportional to the amount of money you will ever make in your life."

The number of people you serve is directly proportional to the amount of money you will ever make in your life. You are on the journey to knowing who you are so that you can identify the unique experiences that only you can create. It is the delivery of this experience (whether in sales or work or creating) that you will exchange for good money.

"You are on the journey to knowing who you are so that you can identify the unique experiences that only you can create."

Now let's go back to where we digressed from; 'look at your father' (I think we are about to digress again). Some people have more than one 'Fathers' so you have to look at all of them. The fact that you have more than one "father' is already separating you from other people. Look at your biological father. Study him, his choices, and his patterns. What are his fears? What is fantastic about him? Therein is a key to your nature.

Look at the 'father' or 'father figure' that trained you, even the ones you silently admired. How did they handle their life affairs? Because therein lies an essential part of your nurture. Everyone has one father, at least.

"Look at your Father(s)... how did they handle their life affairs? Because therein lies an essential part of your nurture. Everyone has one father, at least."

My biological father is a Medical Doctor who came from a proud prominent family in Osu, Ijeshaland of southwest Nigeria in West Africa. He is very brilliant and very charismatic. And he married many wives - my mom is the known fourth.

The foundation of marrying my mom was unplanned at best, and my mom was opinionated and naive, so I was raised technically by a single mother. Long before I grasped the concept of polygamy, I had consistently been sad about us not having a picture of my Dad and Mom in wedding clothes and pose. And when I asked my mom about it as a five-year-old, she told me to ask my Dad the next time I see him.

My Dad worked as a Doctor in Riyadh, Saudi Arabia. Before then, he taught medicine at the University College Hospital Ibadan and when he came home (to Ibadan, Nigeria) which was barely once a year for a few weeks at most, he still had to shuttle between three wives, two others were not in Nigeria. So I rarely saw him yet I loved him, oh my!

I did love my Dad! I saw my Dad for maybe only four hours every year; sometimes I struggled to remember what he looked like. After a while, I would know when he was due to come to Nigeria as I realized that I always dreamed of him weeks before I see him.

Needless to say that looking at my Dad, I understand how and why I am intelligent and want to impart other people, why I am sensitive to people's needs, how I am empathetic, strong and like to teach, why I am independent and children-loving. My absent father/ my father being absent is the sole reason fatherhood is extremely important to me; I am a family man.

"Take a deeply insightful look into your father!"

You would remember that in the movie "Lion King", when Simba was asked this same question he had to look for (at) his father, and only when he had looked at his father could he say I am Simba son of Mufasa. These things are always interesting and underlining everything in amazing ways. In the first of the Kungfu Panda series it seemed like an accident that the Panda was the chosen one, he was definitely the least likely and qualified. And on the third of the series, he had to go find his father.

The father is the strongest and most defining source of identity for the child. Take a deeply insightful look into your father!

Your Mother

Look at your mom and mother figure(s). (My heart goes out to everyone who didn't meet their mom or live with their mom). You have to know that your journey and everything you are, could be and could have already started there. Remember our discussion above about people who didn't know their dads, everything there can be applied to you as well. My mom is a Yoruba woman from Igede-Ekiti [Igede is the town source for the river Osun after which another Nigerian Southwestern State is named]. It is how Nigeria's River Niger came from the country called "Niger Republic".

"A long look at your mother will allow you to understand what your deep-seated fears are and how to conquer them."

My Mom was strong, fearless and courageous. You would be right to describe her as a lioness. She had to function as both Mom and Dad, and she was bothered mostly about how I would turn out, because of the not so silent rivalry between my father's wives.

"Everything in life is expressed in an undeniable pattern, the earlier you understand the pattern of your life the earlier you become advantaged."

All those years of my mom raising me culminated in me becoming responsible. I longed for her to say that she loved me frequently; something that my siblings and I eventually taught her to do. Now she says it a lot.

Shout out to all Millennials of Africa who have started raising children, I know we tell our children how much we love them all the time. My mom is a teacher, and she still teaches Chemistry as I write this. She was hardworking and consistent. She farmed, started a small school, served well in a local church and she prayed a lot. Do I need to tell you that I am bold, courageous, enterprising, a farmer and that I pray a lot? Not for material things; those are settled but I do pray for people and the situations that may have impacts on them. A lot of times I pray when it is the only thing I can do.

A long look at your mother will allow you to understand what your deep-seated fears are and how to conquer them. Everything in life is expressed in an undeniable pattern, the earlier you understand the pattern of your life the earlier you become advantaged.

The People That Loved You

The growth and development of a child is dependent on the love the child gets. You may think that the love needed for the growth of a child is left to cruel chance, hardly is it ever so, you may need to rethink. Let's go back to you knowing yourself.

"You see love is a connection, and love is a mirror; seeing yourself in a little child builds a strong connection and a strong feeling inside of you."

Look at the people that loved you. I am talking about the first set of loves of which you were sure. Some of us were not even sure that our parents loved us, (needless to say why we want our children to know every step of the way and be sure that we love them).

Why should you look at the first set of people that loved you as you grew up? You see love is a connection, and love is a mirror; seeing yourself in a little child builds a strong connection and a strong feeling inside of you.

For me, it was first my late maternal grandmother - Christianah Abimbola Adedipe [Nee Fagbuji]. I met her mother too, by the way. She loved me in ways that I cannot begin to explain; she loved me so much that I still miss her several years after her death. She loved me because she sees a lot of herself in me. Now I know that she saw that I had an uncanny ability to see the best of everything, that I carried a strong light of optimism and believe the best of people all of the time. I look at her, and I see me. I am an optimist.

"I look at her, and I see me. I am an optimist."

For me, it is also my late Uncle Olusola Olatunji Adedipe also known as Sholay Dipson. My eyes well with tears as I remember him right now, he loved me, and he was so proud of me. I was a little boy [what could I have possibly achieved?] - He was proud of me just for existing. He carried me around and flaunted me everywhere he went.

Bro Sola, as we fondly called him, wove much of the foundation of my male [gender] confidence into me, and I didn't even know it. He was a dreamer and a storyteller; Uncle Sola. I still remember those stories you told me, I bet you'd be prouder of me now. I am now a Doctor of Vet Medicine, who has IT and Real Estate Companies. I do miss you a lot. And yes, I grew up into a fine young man just as you thought I would. I am a dreamer too, and I tell beautiful stories. I look at you, and I see me.

Your Earliest Memories

Recall your first memory(ies) and look at them, I am going to share two of my own earliest memories, for whatever reason, these memories stood out. This was the first outing of my consciousness, life began. I am not sure how old I was, but I was certainly less than three years. It must be my core person picking and distinctively identifying things in my environment that resonated with who I am, and this was long before I even knew my name.

"I realized very much later in life that I loved humanity and wanted every way to better the lot of humanity... I am a change agent no matter how much I hide."

I was probably in a crèche, a place not as fancy as the word I used to describe it. I don't remember who took me there or how I left there every day. I have no memory of what I was taught there or what we did there, but this particular day, there was a noise downstairs, the crèche was upstairs we all rushed to the balcony; other crèche children and I, to be let in on the why.

It happened that a goat had fallen into a well, the well seemed to me to lack proper covering the way I remember it. It was a pregnant black goat, the goat yelled out from inside the well. I don't remember seeing the details of how the goat was rescued but I am not going to forget ever. I remember feeling very sorry for the goat and very afraid for every human who could fall inside the well.

I realized very much later in life that I loved humanity and wanted every way to better the lot of humanity. I remember wondering why there had to be a well that someone could fall into, or why wells had to be made in a way goats or people could fall into it. I am a change agent no matter how much I hide.

"That was how I subconsciously knew that there was something called the pain of process to birth great things or become a great person. So I am a man of process."

My second memory was about my mom refusing me sleep and flogging me over some simple counting or Arithmetics. Her mom couldn't bear my crying and she tried rescuing me, but my mom overpowered her mom, and I couldn't be rescued. I had to get what I was being taught. That experience opened my academic journey on a new path. That was how I subconsciously knew that there was something called the pain of process to birth great things or become a great person. So I am a man of process.

Recall Your Growing Up

I was barely ten when mom and dad fought. Dad instructed mom to take us and go live in Osu; the small town that we hailed from. I had a time mixing with the people of my origin, and I thought it was awful because I was coming from such an urban setting as Ibadan. Now it happens that a lot of my good friends come from there, including one of the very best friend 'person' I ever got to know. "See People" as he is fondly called.

The people are amazing and I learnt many things about my lineage than my dad was ever at liberty to share with me. In the future when I contest for the gubernatorial seat in my state, the Osu people will be the reason I stand any chance of winning, and I would be their pride.

"I ended up knowing how to connect with people in the blink of an eye, and now I am adept at making acquaintances. I am a people person, and I crave stability."

What was growing up like for you? I was bitter about it for a while but now I am happy that I lived at Osu for more than six years. I spent most of my teenage years there. I ended up attending 12 different schools in thirteen years. It was almost as though I was never going to know stability, I had to make new friends every time. I ended up knowing how to connect with people in the blink of an eye, and now I am adept at making acquaintances. I am a people person, and I crave stability.

It just occurred to me now that however uncommon it may seem, there may be people who never had any major challenge while growing up. If you are one of those people, you are goals; you have to help us find out how and why, and you have to come and teach the whole world what you or most likely your parents knew that made it possible to create such a perfect life for you. Wouldn't that be an intriguing story?

Your Growth Curve

Pay attention to your growth, what are the growth curves or junctions of your life. And I suppose if I shared mine, it might help you identify yours. What were the experiences that preceded the times in your life when you experienced exponential growth? What things led to those experiences? When were the times that you feel that your growth stalled the most? What things did hinder your growth? I have had several growth curves, as you have also had.

My growth always came every time I expressed myself; it happened to me in my two hundred level days in the University of Ibadan when I started to talk and write. I met more people and made some real friends that I have until now. I became more relevant, and it led to a lot of other beautiful things that happened to me at the University of Ibadan. The exciting thing about my writing then was that it was merely my ungarnished view of our undergraduate life as vet students.

Another growth curve of mine was when I started acting, another form of expression. I met more people; I created some of the memories I would tell my great-grandchildren. Another growth curve came for me at the National Youth Service Corps Orientation Camp when I put myself out, talking and participating, it was at Ede, Osun State Batch 2013B. I was offered my first job because I participated in a professional proficiency HR class.

All my excellent growth curve followed when I launched out and expressed myself. I know this book is preceding another massive growth curve for me and consequently for you. I look at my growth (curves), and I see that I am a giver and a person who loves to share.

"...I see that I am a giver and a person who loves to share."

I found out that my growth stunted every time I tried to follow normalcy and security. My growth stunted every time I was afraid to launch (out). My growth stalled every time I hid. My growth stunted every time I was scared of venturing. Now, I know that I am an eagle, and I was made for the skies. I flew every time I spread my wings and fell every time I perched for too long.

Another important truth about growth is that it hardly happens in the comfort zone, it would oftentimes require that you step out and overcome some sort of inertia. It may also require that you think less of what people may think or say about you or about why, when, where and how you want to venture.

"Another important truth about growth is that it hardly happens in the comfort zone, it would oftentimes require that you step out and overcome some sort of inertia."

Most minds have learnt smallness, they may be unable to comprehend, accommodate or cheer you on.

What story does your growth curve tell? What are you being pointed to?

Your Belief

You will not be the first person that needs to have faith; there are too many things out of the reach and control of one single mind for that mind not to want or have faith. Like you, I need to believe that there is some person, a universal mind who knows and can identify me from the billions of other people and is interested in me doing pretty well.

"This is me speaking for me; I do not speak for you. I do not know what you believe, but you have to check."

For me, it is the Christian God and its divine trinity. I was born into the Christian religion, but I have also independently evaluated all the proposals of the most popular religions. I looked at religion as though they were proposals from powerful entities. And I have decided that I love the Christian God. I believe that He gave his son who had always been a spirit to die in the human form, a way for the Christian God to feel firsthand what it felt like to be human (our frailty and futility), of course, I also believe that he raised His son from death. I believe that the Christian God also manifests as a third person - the Holy Spirit that it is in this form that He can abide with me, the way nitrogen and oxygen abide together in the atmosphere all the while you breathe.

I evaluated the proposal of the Christian God Spirit. He says he wants me to be a legitimate child of His, and He went through the process of paying and legally claiming me as His child so that I can boldly call myself the same and claim every of my inheritance without being unsure if I was indeed His child.

"What you believe will shape what you expect and what you fear. What you expect, has a way of attracting you and what you fear has a knack for happening to you."

Other proposals by my judgment are not quite as good. None offered me divinity, and none categorically love. I also imagined that all religions were a scam, so I went with the one that I believe is best crafted. I am rewarding the 'effort' put by one almighty God into loving me, after seeing all that He went through. I believe and love Him back. This is me speaking for me; I do not speak for you. I do not know what you believe, but you have to check.

Thrilling thing is that you have the right to change or upgrade what you believe. I have sons, and I know that they do not have to do anything to become my sons; they already are.

You may want to consider believing right or at least believing best. What you believe will shape what you expect and what you fear. What you expect, has a way of attracting you and what you fear has a knack for happening to you.

I believe that there is a sovereign God who is very wise and loves me. I believe that he speaks to me and gives me directions through the nudges of my heart. I have made peace with not understanding everything right now; I will understand it better by and by, and at the end of times.

Who and what do you believe?

Your Dreams

In my mid-teenage years, I suddenly noticed that I had stopped dreaming when I slept. It soon started to bother me; it was weird and disconcerting. Something is wrong with me, I thought to myself, and I had no idea of who or what would help me. One day I heard a prominent man Tunde Bakare said on TV that the most crucial kind of dreams were not the ones you dreamt with your eyes closed but the ones that came with you wide awake. I rested from my anxiety and focused on the dreams I dreamed up by myself.

I wanted to make the world better; I wanted to give hope and alleviate poverty (in West Africa). My dreams are valid, and they are beginning to come through. I am my dreams. Your dreams are valid too because they are you. One day without knowing exactly when it resumed I realized I had begun to dream again during sleep. Your daydreams scare your worst nightmares, use them well.

"My dreams are valid, and they are beginning to come through. I am my dreams. Your dreams are valid too because they are you."

Your Miracles

What do you miraculously know? There may be big scientific words to explain intuition or the I-just-knew-it complex. You can query and research how that came to be, but at the end of the day, it is what it is.

In a bid to know who you are, you have to diligently consider the things that you know that somehow you do not remember ever being taught. These things could cut across several things. I began to notice that I just sort of always know how things could be better, or how things could work better, Enore my wife would say *"baby you always know what you should or what a person should do"*. I deal in solutions to complex problems. You have to bring to remembrance all those things that you always "just knew". They are certainly an inkling into who you are.

"You have to bring to remembrance all those things that you always "just knew". They are certainly an inkling into who you are."

Your Gifts

Insight is a gift, so is the ability to design, expressions [art, music, etc.], and understanding of deep things and issues, are gifts which uncannily manifest. Optimism is also one of my many gifts. Your gift(s) is /are an integral part of who you are. I argue alongside the people who say everyone has talents, you may have shut yours out or down but, it is time for you to

35

rediscover it, and to do that you simply need to pay attention from this point in your life on.

"Don't be too broke that you can't pay attention"

Your Joys and Sadness

Humans were not engineered to be helpless. It just isn't part of your makeup. You are not helpless. Pay attention to everything that makes you feel helpless; it is telling you something, decipher it. What gives you kicks, what form moments for you, unforgettable moments? What makes you come alive? What makes your eyes sparkle?

People, that is what makes my eyes glitter, I love people, anything that makes people happy gives me joy-directly relating with people, especially people whom I believe have the opportunity to do, know and make better choices than I made.

For some people, it is arts and creating music. Now you understand when I say I am a mentor of people with diverse gifts. I have accompanied many people on the journey of discovering themselves. I am journeying with you now too (you don't know, that SH*T is better than ecstasy, imagine how happy I'd be when you start to send your video feedback to our social media pages.

Please use the hashtag **#MakeYourMoneyFindYou** so that we may find you easily).

"Pay attention to everything that makes you feel helpless; it is telling you something, decipher it."

Pay attention to feelings that you could never explain away no matter how much you tried, what feelings could you never shake off? You need to start taking those very seriously. Needless to say that I derive joy from helping other people discover themselves (Everyone derives satisfaction from assisting other people, the question is how do you help other people?).

What You Give

I think I want to rephrase that to what people get from you when it comes to active and intentional giving. It is only the people who know who they are that can readily say what they give out to the people who interphase with them. For persons still trying to answer the question of who they are, they can use knowing what people get from them as a mirror in which they can see themselves.

If people find it easy to tell you things about themselves and confide in you, then people get confidence or trust or empathy from you. People may find you very inspiring; you are an inspiration. You just need to look closely, or you may take a survey where you ask your associates, 'what do you get from me?'

"People may find you very inspiring; you are an inspiration. You just need to look closely..."

Your Experience

Your experience is a big part of who you are; this is always as unique as your DNA because when you run two people through the same series of events at the same time, different things will jump at the two of them at different times; this is why some people can take-make photographs while some people cannot.

Long-time ago when my friend Kay and I, watched movies together, he would notice camera angles, why and when they zoomed out or in, he would marvel at the dexterity of the directors [I am convinced now that a movie Director is asleep somewhere inside him] while I was always carried away with the experience of the words and the effects they created, the depth and mystery of the story. I am sure you know why some of us can appreciate Mangas and Animes like Naruto and The FullMetal Alchemist. God bless those writers. Please pay attention to the things that you appreciate they are a clear window into who you are.

Detours; The Interesting Thing About Them

Another angle to this experience thing is the lesson angle, and this is the point where I need to discuss the issue of forgiving yourself, guilt forces a head down and makes it difficult for the owner of the head to see his/her own way. It seems difficult to accept that the stupid things you inflicted on yourself can have purpose or meaning. Guilt wants to kill you, do not allow it. Forgive yourself, Make peace with yourself, cry (I do not care if you are male or female or unsure) yourself to tears, beg you to forgive you and then forgive yourself.

"Don't treat detours or getting lost as a terrible thing; detours are the best things that can happen to a person."

There are many ways to get to where you are going. You are where you are supposed to be. If you do not know where you are, chapter 3 talks about the compass and the GPS with which you will locate yourself. Don't treat detours or getting lost as a terrible thing; detours are the best things that can happen to a person.

At the very worst, you will learn lots of lessons from it, but usually, you will always get more from the experience. If you allow yourself, you will meet the best friends of your life; you may find the love of your life; you will find protégés and mentors that will change your life forever.

"He found everything he needed to win in life on a detour."

We all like to watch movies, and some of us are in tune with the child inside of us, so we still watch a lot of animations. So in 2006, Pixar Animation Studios made this computer-animated road-comedy film (the film was acquired and released by Walt Disney Pictures though) that grossed over four hundred and sixty-two million dollars from a budget of one hundred and twenty million dollars. The Anime is Car, and it is about how everything Lightning McQueen - a rookie needed to win the Piston Cup but much more was his unplanned detour to Radiator Springs. He found a mentor and coach who had won the Piston Cup thrice. Mater, his biggest fan and best friend, and Sally the love of his life. He found everything he needed to win in life on a detour.

Every rookie will get his or her detour, and by the way, aren't we all rookies in life? We all just got here, no one can prove that he has been to 'life' before.

Never forget that however unpleasant your experiences may be and feel at first, they are (fantastic) gifts to you. If only everyone knew that their detours are where they will find more than everything they need to win.

Most people cannot comprehend how a brutal mistake of theirs can be a blessing; you better accept that the universe has a way of leading you to where you are supposed to be at the moment you are supposed to be there, as said in "Men In Black" movie.

"You may get stuck or lost in the detour if you do not want to learn, observe and accept it as a gift."

Car was nominated for two Academy Awards but lost to another animated film -Happy Feet - it is about a penguin who wanted to tap dance where everyone was supposed to sing. It turns out that he would later win his mate and save the entire Royal Emperor Penguin race with tap dancing.

Detours can become painfully long, if you do not learn the lessons that you were supposed to learn as accurately and precisely as you should. You may get stuck or lost in the detour if you do not want to learn, observe and accept it as a gift.

Chapter 3

The Trap: Losing yourself

Born Lost: The Conformers

Some people never really find themselves or have to find themselves because there were not so many reasons to do so. Having a job and joining the 'normal' struggle may have dulled your need to be who you were meant to be. At best, you make tales about your experience at the bar when you hang out with your friends to drink or when at the salon. You say your own experience because the gist is hot and you are feeling left out. You are part of the system, and because you are a tiny part of the system, you may not be able to see the system precisely for what it is.

"You are part of the system, and because you are a tiny part of the system, you may not be able to see the system precisely for what it is."

I am going to tell you a story, but before I do, there is an excerpt from a letter written several decades ago to people like you that you must see.

"Do not be conformed (fashioned after and adapted) to this world system (its external, superficial customs, this age...)" Paul 0005BC

The Matrix

When the world was about to hit another Millennium, two brothers gave the world a movie gift (later to be a trio gift), the world stood at a standstill to receive The Movie "Matrix", this was long before Keanu Reeves was acclaimed with John Wick Film Series. Matrix carried a coded message for you.

In the movie, the world had fallen, an aftermath of a bloody human war with artificial intelligence, even the sun had blacked out, and the little remnant of the human race had retreated and drilled close to the earth's core for energy and safety. Sentinels patrolled the surface of the planet looking to annihilate any trace of human life.

The machines needed energy sources, they soon found out that the human body was a viable unlimited energy source, they called us batteries, and it was not difficult to artificially inseminate and grow baby in tubes, it was not also difficult to feed the human body all through it life, each 'battery' provided energy in thousand folds to what it cost in energy to make, service and feed it. The machines soon had a deadly problem; the human batteries were dying in droves at an age that under normal circumstances, would have been the onset of their consciousness.

It was the human mind causing the problem; the body could not exist without a mind that was engaged, so they created a computer-based Virtual Reality Programme called the Matrix. The bodies would be in pods, sleeping, breathing, feeding and immobilized. The mind will be plugged into the complex and brilliant matrix system, the mind will grow and experience everything in there; the mind will be guided to make choices already programmed for it. All the while the mind will never see that it is in a matrix... I am going to stop the story here, you should go get the movie and watch.

Ill At Ease

Most of the minds in the matrix never knew anything was wrong, but some minds just kept having weird feelings about how the whole system was rigged, sounds familiar to you? The movie may have been a sci-fi, but you have to realize that we are indeed within a system. It is what the letter refers to as this world's system; the system was designed to enslave you.

The system was designed to make it impossible for you to live your true dreams. The system was created to frustrate you. The system will take your dreams, to sell it back to you at the cost of your entire life, leaving you wondering what the point of everything is. It is the question of what the point of everything is that has driven many people to take their own lives; the world's system had overwhelmed their minds so much that they had lost meaning.

I am sending you light and love and hope now, every one of you who have had or have suicidal thoughts, things can get overwhelming, and it feels a lot like drowning - my heart goes out to you now. This book will help you find meaning and hence find yourself. I want to hear and help you share the story of how you overcome. Please DM me on my social media @amoluayoola everywhere.

The World's System

Now you understand why the letter instructed that you must refuse to be conformed; if you have been living in a pod it is time to wake up. You have to see the system for what it is. The world system forces you to focus on the things that are of no lasting importance, to take your focus off what the true essence of life is, you must resist it with everything you have, you must renew your mind, and you must feed your mind with positive life words and thoughts. Thoughts are the recipes, corresponding words are the cooking.

The World system are things like office opening hours, bank closing times, admissions merit systems into universities, pay grades, insurance systems, retirement ages, gender pay gap, what is politically correct, policymaking, news and media agencies, the narrative that they force you to listen to, what days are weekends, what times are holidays, what Jesus looks like and much more. Have you ever wondered why as important as money is, making it is not a subject in our school curriculums? How weird is that?

Now, recall the names of the world's most wealthy people as you know them, let their faces slide slowly across the screen of your mind, do they look to you like average-within-the-system people? I bet not! Do you think the things that apply to you apply to them? Do they have to make the same queues that you have to make? Do you think the bank closes for them on weekends? Do you think they see money the same way you see it? How do you think they see you?

"Once you open your eyes and see the system for what it is, your journey begins."

Everyone on this level of wealth either feels like a god or like a sage or like he is blessed or like a system hacker. This book is not about how they got there; this book is about how you need not bother about whether your money is trapped in their hands or not. Once you open your eyes and see the system for what it is your journey begins.

Decide What Is Good

The letter continued thus…

"But be transformed [changed] by the entire renewal of your mind [with new ideals and attitude], so that you may prove [for yourselves] what is good and acceptable and perfect…"

There are too many things I can say in this paragraph on this subject but I may want to keep it to just one thought line. Have you ever had any questions as to the importance of money? My guess would be that you have never had questions about the importance of money. We all know and agree that money is a very important part of life.

The world is obviously reeking of too many poor people, every fact and statistics say so. Does it not strike you as strange that money is yet to be introduced into the education curriculum as a subject by itself? Have you ever candidly wonder why or why not?

It is your prerogative to decide what is good (at least for yourself).

Overrated Normal

When you were growing up, did it break your heart that your parents were apart and that your father was a worker who was transferred with little or no recourse for his family life? Did it hurt you to see your mother so lonely? How did you feel seeing your father struggle and yet try to appear to have everything under control? Remember when you saw mom cry, how horrible was it?

"Refusing to be conformed and transforming your mind means you decide what is right and what is wrong, you have that power."

Everyday people shuttle day and night to work so that they earn enough to keep the houses they never actually lived in for more than 8 hours daily. In simple terms, it means you use 16 hours to slave so you can have a place to rest for eight hours so you can go and slave another 16 hours the next day.

Refusing to be conformed and transforming your mind means you decide what is right and what is wrong, you have that power. It is wrong to have children and have to be away from them most of the time to feed them. Even animals fare better.

You can decide that it is wrong for your child to have to pick between having you and having food. You can set new ideals and fresh attitude to life and prove to yourself what is good, acceptable and perfect... your parents and maybe you until now were in the rat race.

The Rat Race:

"This is the rat race, you must know it for what it is, and you must decide that you are going to get out of it."

People work at jobs that they detest, jobs that make them very unhappy. **"Thank God It's Friday (TGIF)"** is not a phrase that comes from a place of purpose or fulfillment. Whatever things rid you of joy and meaning is bad for your soul, whatever is bad for your soul is bad for your health, and whatever wants to kill you is not your friend.

This is the rat race, you must know it for what it is, and you must decide that you are going to get out of it. Getting out of it starts with knowing you are in a rat race in the first place. Getting out is easy once you have a necessary, clear idea of what is right, good, acceptable and perfect.

However, I must state clearly for the benefit of all, that most of the things people refer to as "bad" "cruel" and being in a rat race are an attitude problem. Attitude is almost everything. Before I go further to discuss the concept of the rat race, I need to discuss the issue of attitude.

A lot of people who work now are not profitable. People work in organizations they do not care about or seek to uphold. A lot of people have not left their jobs because nobody else wants them, on the flip side it means your present job is accommodating you when no one else would accommodate you. You need to imagine what kind of attitude you would expect someone who has no one else but you to have when they are dealing with you.

You are not profitable if you treat your establishment like shit. You are treating your establishment like shit if you do not bring anything to the table. You are not bringing anything net worthwhile if you have to be told all the time what to do. If you are always looking for ways to cut corners on your establishment you are not a good person and so you need to get out of your bad attitude. Remember how it was told that Steve Jobs would fire engineers who were not using Apple PCs over time. He saw that such engineers could never profit Apple.

Your work is not a rat race if you get credit for your work. Your job is not a rat race if you are not competing with other employees for the same pay raise or promotion. Your job is not a rat race if it allows you to spend as much time as you want with your children and spouse. You are not in a rat race if you wake up every Monday morning with excitement, high hopes, and great expectations.

We need to assume for truth that your work is a rat race, life is a race, and you simply don't want to be in a rat race, you want out, you want to be in a good race, but people run in races. Where else would you have been taught how to run at all?

"What I do need to tell you though, is that many people got out of the rat race, so if they did it, you can also 'did' it."

I am going to bring everything you have read in this book from the foreword up to this point together in the last chapter and explain to you how you can get out of the rat race.

I do not need to tell you that the rat race (an integral part of the world's system) was not built so that people can get out of it, you probably already noticed, seeing your old relatives queue for their retirement pension paychecks at the old age of Seventy-five and sometimes above.

What I do need to tell you though, is that many people got out of the rat race, so if they did it, you can also 'did' it. To get out of the rat race you have to let the race add to you, you need to see the rat race as adding to you, not as an establishment that wants to use you. I repeat once again that no one can use you, only you can use yourself. You can only get out of the race when you beat the race, not winning the race, win your greed, win your natural human desires.

The desire to be better than everybody else is futile, the desire to better everyone around you is better. The desire to use people to get things is unwise while the desire to use things to get people is wise. Depending on how you choose to *waka* your *waka*, you may end up building the best of relationships with your colleagues and boss.

There are two kinds of winning people, you may win people based on out-accomplishing them in preset tasks and exercises and you may win their souls based on love, respect, and adoration. What you call a rat race at this period may be grounds for you to learn collaboration.

I am going to round off on this heading by sharing a profound lesson from the good book specifically from the words of Yeshua. Just before I do that, let me tell you that Yeshua is someone you should listen to more often, all the religions of earth agree that he is and by extension his words are most wise and profound.

Yeshua goes thus I am paraphrasing *"you have no business wondering about the methods of your boss, he may even be outright nasty, you are to focus against being redundant you must be profitable."* This is one other essence of Yeshua's parable, I talked more about it in chapter 6 as I explained the concept of having.

Finding Yourself

This chapter was supposed to deal with losing yourself, and I better get right to it. Some group of people have minds who can readily reason the futility of the world's system, and they rebel against the system, refusing to work for any organization. They just ventured into doing their own things. Some of them may be lucky and flourish while some are not as lucky.

Trying to leave the rat race before you know who you are will amount to rebellion. A little history should tell you that the authorities don't do too well with rebelling subjects. Usually, the system will try to make a terrible example of the rebels, to discourage others from thinking of the same line of action. Many people fall in this category, and they suffer, I hope this book finds you on time (if you see this, please encourage your friends to get their copy of this book).

If you leave the system before you know who you are, you are likely not going to be able to stand the financial and family pressure that will follow the challenges of negative cash flow. This is the time that people lose themselves and run back into the rat race, settle for the life of pain and misery.

"Trying to leave the rat race before you know who you are will amount to rebellion."

The second chapter of this book has taught you how to identify yourself, do go find yourself right away. You will be tested, you may almost forget who you are, little success will test you, adversity and opposition will test you, you will have trials, you may lose yourself once in a while, but now that you have read this book you will always have a compass, you will always be able to find you and to turn things around for you and your family. Chapter four will teach about the things you need to do now to set yourself irreversibly on the path to a great life.

To Believe or To Disbelieve.

You have likely heard the word "believe" more than a hundred thousand times in your life already, you have an idea of what it means, you have seen it in movies how the good guys have to keep believing in the face of utmost despair otherwise the movie will have a sombre ending. You have seen it many times in these movies that you do not think highly of it anymore. These things are universal messages to you. I am going to explain this believe concept to you in another manner.

The North Star

Long-time ago people moved around and decided Up (North) Down (South) Right (East) and Left (West) by simply locating the North Star (Polaris) because this star sits very close to the north pole of the planet earth.

Now the North Pole is on the surface of the earth, a location that is covered by ice, it is very much impossible for you to see the North Pole from where you stand for several reasons like the fact that your perfect eyes will converge the horizon at the farthest distance of 1.6 miles. So even if you were to be standing on closest habitable place to the north pole which is about 817KM away, you still would not see where the North Pole is but you can always look up and once you identify the north star you'd know where north is and then you would be able to determine what direction you need to go.

"You see, the truth will always remain the truth…, it will always be there even though you may not be able to see it physically or evidently. The truth is that you will succeed."

You see, the truth will always remain the truth; in this analogy, the truth is the North Pole, it will always be there even though you may not be able to see it physically or evidently. The truth is that you will succeed. Believing the truth is Polaris, the North Star.

As long as you keep believing, you'd never be lost, no matter where you wander to, you can always believe (lookup). By the way, I hope you still remember that to believe is to accept that something is true, especially without physical proof – because it is easy for anyone to accept the physical proof. The most important time to believe is when you are not sure.

"You must never stop believing because a time will come when you will have nothing to hold on to other than what you believe."

What the Rat Race intends to do: the aim of the rat race is to get you to a place where you can no longer accept that it is true that your life was created to matter in the scheme of things. You must never stop believing because a time will come when you will have nothing to hold on to other than what you believe. To stop believing is to get lost. Be prepared for occasional self-doubts; it is part of the package being human. You may not at this time look like the truth that you believe, but if you hold on to the North Star, you will never get lost, instead you will get to where you are going. Your physical reality will soon align with your strongest belief, you will soon get to where you are going. If it ever gets dark, please look up and find your north star.

"To stop believing is to get lost. Be prepared for occasional self-doubts; it is part of the package of being human."

An Interesting GPS System

The Trio of Love, Faith, and Hope: Things are much better now, it is not likely that anyone carrying a powered device such as a phone will ever be lost, thanks to the GPS, the GPS works in a simple way. At every point you stand on the surface of the earth there are always at least three satellites hovering over you at 20,000KM away beaming signal to you at the speed of light. Your device picks signal from the closest satellite to you first and picks signal from the farthest of the three satellites last your device knows the speed of light so it can calculate how far each moving (orbiting) satellites is, in a matter of milliseconds your device can see the arc line of movement of each of the satellites. Your device pinpoints your location by determining where the three lines intercept.

Your Three Satellites

Your orbiting satellites are Love (an intense feeling of affection), Faith (the alignment of actions, words, and conviction), and Hope (an intense feeling that good things will come. Have Love, faith, and hope; and you will see that you can never be lost.

"...acknowledge and accept all the gifts that life brings your way, the gifts of people, the gifts of experience, the gifts of mistake and the gifts of loss."

You are still growing, and I want you to keep these things in mind. Because you are still growing (you may not even have concluded the first twenty percent of your life's journey and endeavours) life is about to push you to many frontiers. Sometimes you may feel alone and lonely, acknowledge and accept all the gifts that life brings your way, the gifts of people, the gifts of experience, the gifts of mistake and the gifts of loss.

Love, Faith, and Hope

You must never be found wanting in love, faith, and hope. Your words and actions must constantly and consistently align with your deepest convictions; this is faith, it is what they mean when they say "may your aim be true". Faith allows you to create good realities with your words, faith energizes and helps you to pursue your dreams in the face of 'nothing is promised or certain'.

Hope allows you to be radiant so that you can inspire and charge the people around you with strength and radiance, hope allows you to expect good things. Good things happen and bad things happen, hope helps you make the best of your expectations. Love allows you to give and love allows you to accept. Giving and not accepting will bleed you dry, accepting and failing to give will choke you. Love allows you to access and see the gifts very few will see.

I am sure you are familiar with the idea of directions, moving from a geographical point A to Point B. The whole system of navigation and reference relies on very few constant things like the North Pole. Never forget love, faith and hope they are your GPS, use them as frequently as you need.

Chapter 4

Nobody Can Make Your Money
**"Because of your unique experience, only you
can serve people in the way only you can".**

This means that nobody can give people the exact
experience that you will give them. Your money is
distinct and looking for you, and nobody can make your
money. I am going to address that belief that suggests
that you would never have your own money because it
looks like all the opportunities have been taken.

Nature harbours vacuum; someone is holding your
money for you now. S/he is just there unknowingly
looking for the experience or expression that only you
can provide based on everything God had deposited in
you and everything you have learnt. The universe was
setting you up for greatness every inch of the way.

Don't settle for less. When you are ready, when you
know who you are, when you do who you are without
fears or apologies, when you give yourself, when you
come out, your money will find its way to your pocket.
The world makes room for everything that grows, and
the world always create space for every serious, un-
held back manifestation.

"When you are ready, when you know who you are, when you do who you are without fears or apologies, when you give yourself, when you come out, your money will find its way to your pocket."

What Is The Hardest or Greatest Thing That You Ever Imagined?

Everyone on the planet earth can be rich, you must force your mind to see that possibility; however, it is too much of a task for the untrained mind. You must allow your mind to imagine and see a world where everyone is prosperous.

It is not likely that the world will ever exist, so the essence of the exercise is not to make you create such a world, (I just paused to take in a big dose of music from Adol featuring Yemi Alade, Sekere, using a headphone from a Tecno Camon 11 Phone, can you imagine all the minds that expressed themselves so I can have this experience. Of course you know I paid for them with money, now I am enjoying myself, and you have no idea what it feels like because you are not me) but to create such a world for yourself. It is a serious task, albeit a little difficult, but you must pause now and close your eyes and imagine that world this instant.

"You must allow your mind to imagine and see a world where everyone is prosperous."

Now that you have done it, you need to open the eyes of your mind to possibilities, hope, and greatness. Look at everything you are now; they are things that you once 'saw'; in fact, most of them are things that you did not lose 'sight' of. Now, that begs the question of why did I not ask you to imagine you alone being rich. I did not ask you to do that because it is a seed of selfishness, the selfish mind will eventually stunt and die, and miserably too, and I am not going to allow you go down that path. Secondly, remember that You are You, but You are not about you.

Being all about you is a sure recipe for living a small and inconsequential life. It is not what you can do as much as what you can do for others. So it is not, particularly what you are as much as what you are to others. And the number of people you are something to (whether they know it or not) is the quality of your life. At the very least, you know what Google is to you and what it does for you and billions of other people. I am sure I do not need to remind you that Google founders are Billionaires of the world acclaim.

"Being all about you is a sure recipe for living a small and inconsequential life. It is not what you can do as much as what you can do for others."

The Money Burden

Do you have burdens? Do you think it is your responsibility to lift your family out of poverty? Do you think you owe it to your loved ones to improve the quality of their lives? This is how you will successfully do it without running mad or becoming an embittered SOB.

"Finding you is how to find everything else."

The Financial Implication Of The Society

Belonging to a system cost money, some of this system's cost is necessary and is at the base of Maslow's Theorem. Some other system's cost is point blank unnecessary. You have to know when heaven will fall and when heaven will not fall. You have to be able to separate between when a thing is important and right versus when you are just plain afraid of what people will think if you stand out in whatever way.

I am trying to tell you that there is a financial implication of the society to which you belong. And one sure way to lose yourself is by being afraid, being afraid to stand out, being afraid to stand alone, and being afraid to be different.

Child experts have argued that you were born with two or three fears, that you learned all your other fears. Admit truths and dismiss fears. Easier said than done though, which is why success is for the eagles and not for the chickens. The most successful tale of the chicken is in the cooking pot or the logo of an eatery, I believe you need not be introduced to everything that the eagle stands for. Are you an eagle or a chicken?

"Easier said than done though, which is why success is for the eagles and not for the chickens ...... Are you an eagle or a chicken?"

In my next book which I am likely going to title 'Be Awesome', I am going to expressly explain the concept of courage and the contemporary reality, but I am going to borrow from that book now to tell you that, yes, it will take some degree of courage for you to determine when not to follow the herd.

What do people do or pay for that you do not need to do or pay for? What needs have the society taught you as necessary that truly aren't? Only you can determine those. And while you are at it, please ask yourself 'What am I afraid of?' and if I hold my own, what is the worst that could possibly happen?

"More times than not, life hacks are as simple as watching what everyone else is doing and doing the exact opposite."

If it does not make sense, it does not make sense. That a lot of people do something does not make that thing sensible. Guess who is poor too, a lot of people!

You guessed right. More times than not, life hacks are as simple as watching what everyone else is doing and doing the exact opposite.

People have, some of the time, willingly lost themselves. They dropped their identity and face to become a faceless addition to statistics.

There is nothing wrong with being you, everything is already wrong, people being right is how we are going to fix the world. You are a voice, you are a system, you are your little media and you can inspire others if you just do differently. The world has a lot of machines, data and statistics already, it definitely could use more humans.

Having to bow to every financial burden your social structure brings your way, will make you lose yourself as you would be forced into the rat race or forced to cut corners. None of these choices are good, none of them will serve you in good stead.

Were You Promised

Did you grow up with everyone telling you you were going to become a Doctor? Don't blame them. That was on a light note. A lot of people grew up hearing words like "this one is special," "she is different", "he is the best of your children", "there is something about this one", "this child has a lot of 'glories', lol" and so on... I have a few things to say that I have no particular arrangements for.

"...if they never told you that, you are lucky, you are very lucky, you have

dodged several bullets of expectations, expectations can kill..."

One; if they never told you that, you are lucky, you are very lucky, you have dodged several bullets of expectations, expectations can kill, all the time the most unlikely people are the most successful, I am very happy for you, because it means you can hide your head and create greatness.

Two: if you are a 'promised child' still take your time, make them forget you were promised, go live life, travel, learn and meet people.

There was once a promised child called Yeshua, they said he was going to be the world's greatest child prodigy, well he didn't show up until he was already thirty and certainly no longer a child.

Time is a human construct to make sense of events, you must deconstruct time for yourself if you can. If you cannot, then you must focus on your growth and your journey. Pay little regard to time. You wouldn't need time if you will respect a baby as much as you would defer to an old man. You wouldn't be needing time if you knew what to do and was doing it. You would not be needing time if you spend it on living because you will always have a lot of it.

You Are Still Growing

Time would matter less if you focus on being who you are. More than half the population of people who know Elon Musk can agree that he is a great man. Now, that man had always been Elon Musk. There was a two-year-old Elon Musk as there was an eighteen-year-old Elon Musk. Now, in clear nomenclature terms, none of the two was more Elon Musk than the other. However, you certainly do feel - like everyone else - that right now, Elon Musk is more Elon Musk than ever. This is what life's journey is about, becoming more you than ever. Every time you didn't own your journey you become less of you.

"This is what life's journey is about, becoming more you than ever. Every time you didn't own your journey you become less of you."

You are still growing, you are still becoming. As you go on in life you need a strong internal structure, what some people call a strong sense of self, which means to know that you are different and have a purpose, that you are not a generic product that just has a batch number. To know that not everything that applies to everyone applies to you and that the things that apply to you do not have to apply to other people.

"...you need a strong internal structure...To know that not everything that applies to everyone applies to you and that the things that apply to you do not have to apply to other people."

Chapter 5

The Necessary Internal Structure

Critical Points

To take being misunderstood without being bitter, to do without needing to impress, to understand the need and urgency while you understand rest and ease are all very important in your journey. They are factors to leaving a great life and you deserve to live a great life. You should live a great life!

Every form of success is a weight, weights can kill as well as build capacity. A strong internal structure is how success will not corrupt or deform you.

One necessary internal structure is knowing what to do and being able to do what you want to do without making enemies or judges of people around you.

"Every form of success is a weight, weights will kill or build a person's capacity. A strong internal structure is how success will not corrupt or deform you."

You demonstrate that you have a strong internal structure when you can stop time in its tracks, bend events (the ones that concern you) to your will (you are not likely going to be able to stop the concept of weekdays and weekends just yet).

Sometimes you have to freeze time and bid the world to stop. It happens for every great person, they stop time! I bet it happened and happens for every big name that millions of people in the world know - Obama for example - and this is necessary from time to time. As the world goes, it may become too fast for you. You must learn to slow it down in the quietness within you and sometimes force it to an outright stop, where nothing matters except that which you need to bring forth.

"As the world goes, it may become too fast for you. You must learn to slow it down in the quietness within you and sometimes force it to an outright stop, where nothing matters except that which you need to bring forth."

Of course, time will not literally stop and people will not stop going on with their lives, but what you must do is block them out. You may have to be in solitary, you may appear crazy, it comes with the package , but the world needs you, and you must find you, it is very important. At this time, your only stimulus must come from what you want and need to create.

This is necessary diligence, otherwise your desires and the hopelessness of your inability to create them will almost kill you - what many call 'depression'. This is a major cause of depression and true insanity.

"Your job/concern is not to be normal, your job/concern is to be whom you are... and create an experience or expression from it using whatever legitimate/moral tool that is necessary and appeals to you."

Normal is the definition of what everyone sees everyday. Your job/concern is not to be normal, your job/concern is to be whom you are, to take your passion, skills, experience, and DNA and create an experience or expression from it using whatever legitimate/moral tool that is necessary and appeals to you. In this time you will find out what truly matters to you and you will stop bothering about what does not matter.

"Seeing other people's success may stir up envy in you, but you will see within you that you are truly happy for them."

This is when you will learn to truly be happy for other people. Envy is a natural and spontaneous part of human nature just as much as rain is a natural phenomenon, but when it rains, a house with its roof intact is dry inside.

Seeing other people's success may stir up envy in you, but you will see within you that you are truly happy for them. You will be able to wish them well, knowing that they are not you and therefore are not making your money.

People Making Similar Money To Yours

It is very likely that after knowing who you are, you will see people making money similar to yours, this is where you will learn true humility; humility helps to know that you are not everything, and that there will always be a lot to learn, and that no one knows and is everything.

This is when you will realize that you are enough and adequate, that you already have everything that you need, and that no matter what, you will always have everything that you need at every point in your life you just have to look around you and your relationships with more of gratitude and humility.

This is where you will learn why it is important that you treat people well, that no one can truly use us. It is just plain impossible.

"Your life is proof of things either happening for you or to you and you are the determinant of which."

You are the only one who can use you and this happens when you fail to learn and own everything that has happened to you. The world if filled with several experiences of mistreating people and setting them up for the time of their lives, thinking they were selling them short. It's all there in the good book, in the fairy tales and in the movies. There are also millions of people whose dreams were shattered because they thought the whole world was against them.

When you own your experiences and your journey you are saying that things happen for you, but when you do not accept your experiences or think poorly of your journey, what you are saying, directly or indirectly is that things are/have been happening to you.

"Your life is proof of things either happening for you or to you and you are the determinant of which."

The salient truth is that only you can determine which it is for you. The good news is that in the order of life, it works as though it is a bank deposit made in your name, you can treat experiences as cash deposits and bank drafts drawn against your name or as slander on your person. These deposits will always be there, and when you are ready you can just decide to make as much withdrawal as you need from that wealth of deposit. Just imagine all that you could do if you saw your experiences as a wealth of deposits.

"The good news is that in the order of life, it works as though it is a bank deposit made in your name... Just imagine all that you could do if you saw your experiences as a wealth of deposits."

Building A Strong Internal Structure

Being At Peace

The world is in chaos, it is a place of strife and adversity, but it is also a place of beauty and a place of joy. You can find so much happiness in life if you just allow yourself to.

"You can find so much happiness in life if you just allow yourself to."

This is what you must do - you must make peace everywhere possible. You must make peace with how you got here. Making peace sometimes require that you forgive yourself, please forgive yourself. It is okay to do so. Yes, you may not have done as much as you think you should have. You may not be particularly proud of yourself right now, it's okay, you will soon be.

Make peace with how you got here, make peace with everything that got you here, forgive everyone who 'messed' your life up. Find peace, make peace and be at peace. Where you are certainly leads to where you should be, it does!

"Where you are certainly leads to where you should be, it does!"

Being Unbothered

A lot of things will still happen, things that have the capacity to bother you. Do not let things get at or to you, do not let things bother you till you lose your peace. Do not worry. Another excerpt quotes thus "Do not let your heart be troubled". Do everything you can do, sometimes it won't be enough, sometimes it is never supposed to be. Do not worry! I know you have heard this several times but I am telling you again because one of the keys to building a strong internal structure is to learn to be unbothered.

"One of the keys to building a strong internal structure is to learn to be unbothered."

Being Unperturbed

While this may sound similar to the above, this is what I want you to pick from this paragraph; being unperturbed means seeing through life challenges. And believe me when I say life challenges aren't particularly see-through friendly, but you must see through the challenges and know that a happy ending awaits you.

I had this friend in college, Derin. Together, we were going through some terrible years of academic challenges and he'd always say in pidgin English "everything go kiss" he meant that everything will finally make sense and come to a sensible, meaningful and prosperous end. I believed him and it became something that I have said to myself ever since then. (Adekunle Aderinto, thank you so much).

Being Grateful

We all just kind of know that gratitude is a good thing, especially if we were the ones who did the good deeds. So we truly know how it makes us feel, when someone shows us gratitude. But gratitude is an attitude and it is beyond mere words, of course, we do use words to express gratitude.

Gratitude is more than what we do when someone does something wonderful for or to us. It is a mental position that we all should take. It is like saying that we identify with great things. It is like saying we are candidates for only good things. Grateful must be who you are. Say it out loud to yourself, I am grateful.

"Gratitude is more than what we do when someone does something wonderful for or to us. It is a mental position that we all should take."

Love Life

When fifty people go through the same experiences, few of them in the upper cadre would be very happy, even if the experiences were relatively bad ones. People who have strong internal structure go through life as though they love life, these are the ones we call "always happy".

Your experiences are not the reasons you do love life or not love life, you love life because you decided you would. This a sign from a person who has strong internal structure.

"People who have strong internal structure go through life as though they love life, these are the ones we call "always happy"."

Being Unrushed

I am not referring to sloppy or slothful individuals. Have you seen people who though very efficient and effective, seem to operate with their own (kind of internal) timing?

Haste is never a good sign, at the very best it is a sign of a terrible emergency. People who know who they are often appear as though they cannot be rushed into things, deals or situations.

"Haste is never a good sign, at the very best it is a sign of a terrible emergency."

Chapter 6

Now, Go and Make Your Money

Making Money Versus Making a Living

I am sure that by now you probably have noticed that I have not been/ I am not talking about making small money which is the same thing as making a living. What makes up for your living is the fact that your heart still beats and all of that, the only thing that you need to do for a living is breathe. That is why I took pain to explain the rat race to you and how the world system is not built so you could prosper, how the herd mentality only favors the herder. How you have to get angry with poverty and find yourself.

Kudos to all those who have been making their honest living. If you have been dubious, shame on you, because you can actually be better. I am not judging you though, I am in no place to judge anyone except myself. But now you know what you must do.

Wisdom is profitable to direct, switching to 'making money' from 'making a living' requires wisdom. There are no hard and fast rules as to how to make the switch. It has nothing to do with whether you are on paid employment all your life or not. It has everything to do with whether you pursue your dreams or not. It has everything to do with whether your success is a good success or not. It depends on whether the people who love you see you as frequently as they need to. Whether or not you are everything that you are supposed to be.

It depends on whether you are happy or not. Whether you are living healthy or not. That is what it is about.

"Wisdom is profitable to direct, switching to 'making money' from 'making a living' requires wisdom. There are no hard and fast rules as to how to make the switch."

To get out of the rat race some people have used the swim or drown approach, some people have used the ease-out-of-it approach. The choice is yours. But you definitely have to live your life and that is summed up in whether you serve as many people as possible, whether you deliver experiences or make things only you could have made.

Serve: It's The Magic Wand

Recall how this word has come up in this book severally. I have said repeatedly in this book that the size of your wealth is directly proportional to the number of people that you serve. Build systems of service and products for people. You have to bring to your mind all the 'legitimately' rich individuals that you know in your state or country, can you see the direct correlation between the size of their estate and the number of people that they serve with their systems (Companies).

It is ancient wisdom. One man who lived a long time ago, had his mentees arguing within themselves, they wanted to know who would end up the greatest. "So

Yeshua told them, "look foreign kings and known kings lord their lineage over the people they rule and they call themselves the custodians of order and the peoples' benefactors, you cannot be like that". If Yeshua had come as a millennial he would have sounded like this *"if you do not already come from a royal family it's too late for you to attain greatness using the aristocracy technique and I don't even dig that kind of greatness anyways, if you want to be great you have to behave as though you were the youngest who has the duty to serve, although the one who is served thinks he is better"*

The present age translation of this thousand years old wisdom is that you must build systems that serve people with experiences that make them feel like kings. Yeshua continued saying "but it is a lie the one who serves is greater".

"The present age translation of this thousand years old wisdom is that you must build systems that serve people with experiences that make them feel like kings."

Let me bring this message to a clearer contemporary understanding. Milo beverage of Nestle company [One of the largest companies on the entire planet earth] tells you that you are a champion so you buy lots of milo, a cocoa beverage and you feel good about yourself as you drink a blend of cocoa (a naturally growing plant), milk (something you can get from goats and cattle around you) and sugar (the natural juice of the sugarcane plant). Need I say to you that you are in reality poorer than the real owners of the Nestle Group?

Volunteer To Serve

Intern with the intention to add value while you learn. Internship is another word for insurance over early mistakes. Where else will you find people that will pardon your mistakes and reward your initiatives, not in school and definitely not anywhere else in life?

"Find opportunities to serve, jump at it, learn all the way and then learn some more."

People are afraid that they will be used, I have asked you to settle it in your mind once and for all, and no one can use you as long as you are deliberate and know who you are. Find opportunities to serve, jump at it, learn all the way and then learn some more. Condition your mind to always learn. Learn from everything. There is a lesson in everything. Train your mind to spot lessons fast. Recall lessons regularly.

Give

Give yourself wholeheartedly, give people things, give time, give comfort, give understanding, give heartfelt condolences, give money, give all kinds of material things, live free and uncluttered, empty your closet regularly. Find and take every opportunity to give, give encouragement, give kind words, give support, give attention, give, give and give.

I am going to explain the Christian God science of what happens when you give (willingly, cheerfully and not out of compulsion or from the desire to impress. In fact, the most rewarding gifts are discrete).

You cause an imbalance in the order of things, (the Christian God) the universal mind responds in several ways as is supposed to fit into your utmost purpose and destiny. Sometimes you get similar things easily, other times information of unbelievable deals will mysteriously get to you, sometimes it is your name coming up in influential circles. Giving is a fuel in the engine that drives you forward in life. It is like a cause and effect for miracles. It is how to guarantee good things happening to you. Another thing that giving gets you is goodwill, you need goodwill from as many quarters as you can get them and do not squander them in fits of anger; that would be a foolish thing to do.

"Giving is a fuel in the engine that drives you forward in life. It is like a cause and effect for miracles... Another thing that giving gets you is goodwill, you need goodwill from as many quarters as you can get them."

Everything You Went Through.

Everything you went through can be made better for everyone else at a fair price that they will gladly pay. What gave you sleepless nights? What caused you pain? Could it be your living conditions as an undergraduate? You really can do something about it.

"The person who feels it most is the one who can do the best about it".

Imagine all your countless 'bad' experiences. It turns out that they are actually goldmines. What an interesting irony of life. Sometimes God (The Universal Mind) pays you in ideas for an act of kindness you did (Seyi Faloju, 2011).

"The person who feels it most is the one who can do the best about it. Imagine all your countless 'bad' experiences. It turns out that they are actually goldmines."

Pace Yourself

Haste to get rich will rid you of the experiences that will guarantee your undying wealth, it will rid you of the lessons that you need to pass along to your children as you pass along your dynasty. I am sure that you have heard tales of men who were very rich and had big companies; companies that went bankrupt and dead as soon as they were passed on to their children.

Where I come from, the Yorubas (A tribe in South-West, Nigeria) have a proverb, "Omo t'aa ko a gbe'le t'ako ta". It roughly translates to "the child we fail to train will sell the house we built for peanuts".

Pace yourself does not mean you should be lazy. It simply means that you should understand that your efforts are compounding and may not be immediately visible. Know that everything is adding up as they are also multiplying. A farmer who plants a seed doesn't expect the seed to germinate in a day, much less harvesting it in a day, and depending on what you plant and the volume of harvest, you will give some things time and allow compound effect to work on every effort put into your journey - your success.

"Pace yourself does not mean you should be lazy. It simply means that you should understand that your efforts are compounding and may not be immediately visible."

Pace yourself means, do not be lopsided. Be balanced, function properly across boards, visit and spend time with your grandparents, make your old folks happy, honor your parents, go out of your way for them. Millennials are taking the "independence" drive to a dangerous levels. Don't fall into that trap; "a life lacking the love of people close to you will be both miserable and empty".

"A life lacking the love of people close to you will be both miserable and empty".

The adult life is tough, many things are thrown to you all at once. Please, you have to know what is truly important. Don't be like the people who only realize what is important when they are on their deathbed. Those ones are fools who chased only after shadows all their lives, their wives will remarry their chauffeurs and continue spending their money.

Plan your life and live your life. Sometimes park at the roadside and admire a beautiful sunset, the most beautiful things in life are free. Don't miss them.

"Plan your life and live your life ...the most beautiful things in life are free. Don't miss them."

Have

I have to tell you one of Yeshua's most popular parables, from an unpopular perspective, I think I might even mix two of such parables together. This is the story of capacity before anyone knew to call it capacity.

So this rich master was travelling and so he called his three servants and gave them his goods, he gave the first servant five talents, the second he gave two talents and the third he gave one talent. He gave each of the servants according to what he knew to be their individual ability. So the master went on his journey. Servant A went and traded with the talents for which he gained five more talents on the original five, the second did likewise and also doubled his investments in time but there goes the third servant to bury his master's money.

After a long time the master came home and he called them to report their erstwhile activities, servant A and servant B reported on how they had doubled their talents.

Master says 'well done good and faithful servant' to each of the two servants and added 'now I am going to put you in charge of many more stuff, you are onwards going to be having a time of your life'. Servant C steps forward and says 'Master I know you are a very difficult person, you always expect results from impossible places, leveraging on people and things everywhere, I didn't want any of your troubles Sir so I hid the talent you gave me in the earth, here it is.'

The master now furious replies and says 'you are not just slow and lazy you are also a wicked person, since you knew I had no tolerance for loss or reduction and that I'd rather even benefit from places where I have no input why didn't you just at worst case scenario just put my money in a bank for compound interest, now I would have had some reasonable interest on my money.'

The master commanded the guards to take the single talent from servant C and given to servant A, the one who has a total of ten talents already to make eleven talents. The master says a person who has will get more and surplus and that person who does not have, will lose all that he has to that person who has a lot already. He commands that servant C the unprofitable servant be thrown out of the castle to go live with trolls, LOL. I just had to add that.

I am never going to forget that parable of the talents in a hurry. Did you notice how the master equated being profitable to being faithful? The one servant who didn't add to his talent was themed wicked, slow and unfaithful. I am first very particular about the history that determined why the servants got different counts of the silver. This is where everything begins for you in life, please whatever you do build and acquire capacity. It is not a difficult thing to do, you gain capacity by taking on new responsibilities at every opportunity, putting yourself out there, and doing things. That is how to gain capacity, because one day life, like the master, will want to hand you talents (opportunities) and it will only be able to give you to the size of your capacity.

How much is a talent of silver? A talent of silver according to Wikipedia is 33Kg Silver; which is the equivalent of present day $16,300. This servant had this much but chose to behave like it was nothing. You must decide to have, you must see all that you have. You must acknowledge all that you have with profitable corresponding actions otherwise you are about to lose all that you have to someone who already has too much.

The master came back home after spending a long time on his journey, based on your faithfulness which is your profitability you may not look so different from the people 'playing it safe', but one day all that they kept will become yours.

On your job, give your best, be profitable for your boss. I will say more about this in my next book 'Be Awesome'. One more thing that you should bear in mind is another wise saying of Yeshua that says that "if you have not been faithful (remember that faithful means profitable) in which is another man's, who shall give you that which is your own?" You are never going to create a wonderful life for yourself if you do not create it for other people. I repeat, be profitable in your employers' work this is the only way you are getting out wealthy and meaningfully.

"...whatever you do, build and acquire capacity... because one day life, like the master, will want to hand you talents (opportunities) and it will only be able to give you to the size of your capacity."

Love

Love with all your heart!

you may have some heartbreaks, but love in spite, love recklessly, love well, love with everything you have got, be careful though; do not give pigs your pearl, but love. Love with all your heart and give your heart to beautiful and meaningful causes. When you love, let the whole world know that you did love.

Love is mysterious and very powerful. A heart that does not love is like a ship that never sailed. And if you experience heartbreak, it is a rare opportunity of loving someone who does not want you, watch yourself as you slowly but surely heal. The chest actually aches when you are heartbroken, I remember the feeling very vividly, I experienced it a couple of times. It showed me that I was alive and that I was human.

"Love with all your heart and give your heart to beautiful and meaningful causes. When you love, let the whole world know that you did love."

Love will color your life, giving is often a byproduct of love. Love conquers all. Everything that is made with love is sweeter, better, finer and more appealing. And people can subconsciously tell a product of love apart from the product of indifference. The same for services, and gifts.

And when you want to marry, marry someone who sees you, someone who truly sees you before loving you. You don't want to be in a relationship where your partner cannot see you and you have to scream every time to be seen. I know you understand what I mean

Bless

Bless yourself, bless people, bless everything you can, just bless, bless for fun. This is a rather strange concept. Now, the opposite is the most common, cursing; guess what else is common; poor and unsuccessful people.

Speak good of people, use words that build up, use words that protect, use positive words all the time, to bless a person means to say (declare) good (things)

about the person. Avoid saying bad words with your mouth, because words are very powerful in that they create your realities, they orchestrate the things that you will certainly experience in the future.

"Bless yourself, say good things about yourself, and declare wonderful things about yourself."

Bless yourself, say good things about yourself, and declare wonderful things about yourself. It may be weird at first, but you must never stop saying good things about yourself. Say things like, I am blessed, people love me, I am favored, I am graced, I am prospering, and chances are aligning favorably for me. I go to the right place at the right time. I know what to do at all times. I solve problems, I surmount challenges, I am doing well, and I am making consistent visible and admirable progress.

Words create, I am sure you remember the popular tree experiments. Look at your life right now, you are a product of your fears and your words, as you go through life, conquer your fears by speaking the opposite of them, when you feel weak say that you are strong, when it looks bleak, say you are blessed. When you do not have enough say you have in abundance. Speak a rich language.

Avoid people who curse, mock and slander even for jokes, you can have fun without burning your future.

"Avoid people who curse, mock and slander even for jokes, you can have fun without burning your future."

Where Are You

All of the things above can happen simultaneously, there is no particular sequence. What I am about to write requires that you pay attention. You may have satisfied all of these requirements, they are for your benefits, and these are the things that will determine the quality of your life.

Now, you must look inwards, what would you like to do? What would you like to create? Are you starting it as a sidegig? You know what to do, trust your gut, believe your instinct and you will be fine.

The fear of failing may want to hold you back, but you must not allow that to happen to you, knowing who you are reduces the incidence of shame or stigma, you already know that you are faring better than 80% of the world population who do not even know that they are in a matrix or that they are running a rat race.

"Be fearless, you cannot lose. You will win or learn to win the next time."

Knowing What To Do

A lot of people have asked me how I always know what to do. I tell them I just always knew. There is a little yet very powerful thing called 'listening to your heart'

Do All That You Can

Make up your mind, that you will do all that you can on your venture, that you will do all that you should do. This is important for you, you want to be sure that you have the capacity to see things through and see the end of the matter. This stretches you for growth and increases what you are capable of achieving.

Before You Launch

You may need to learn and unlearn a few things, the learned entrepreneur may have it a bit smoother. In all thy getting, get wisdom… make sure you read on the subjects that matters to your journey, enterprise or dealings.

Some authors Like Robert Kiyosaki and Akin Alabi will help you with a wealth of information and knowledge, you really can start out fine, do well and scale.

The job of this book is not to tell you how to run a business, I may share those in another book of mine where I document my experience at building four different companies. Seek knowledge out, ask questions.

"You may need to learn and unlearn a few things, the learned entrepreneur may have it a bit smoother.' In all thy getting, get wisdom..."

Create, Recreate and Repeat

Create several of the same cycles. Of all the things written above, nothing is linear, most may be happening together at once. This is however not supposed to bother you because you are equipped for it.

As a matter of fact, this is what you should do, you should create more of these cycles of learning, experiencing, serving, giving, loving and setting up business systems because as you have seen, everything is happening for you, now you are equipped for the next phase of your journey. Remember, always pay attention!

In life, many things and many people will unconsciously teach you but you cannot afford to be an unconscious learner.

"In life, many things and many people will unconsciously teach you but you cannot afford to be an unconscious learner".

I am going to close here. I will have you know that you are all you need to have all that you desire to have.

We all have your money in our hands, we will always have it even after we have given you some we can still give you more, if only we see you.

We will not see you if you do not know you. The world is waiting for YOU earnestly because it needs you very badly.

Thank you for reading this book.